MEMORY KEEPER

Author: Holly Garner
Illustrator: Stephanie Miller

an imprint of Sunbury Press, Inc.
Mechanicsburg, PA USA

Copyright © 2025 by Holly Garner.
Cover Copyright © 2025 by Sunbury Press, Inc.

Sunbury Press supports copyright. Copyright fuels creativity, encourages diverse voices, promotes free speech, and creates a vibrant culture. Thank you for buying an authorized edition of this book and for complying with copyright laws. Except for the quotation of short passages for the purpose of criticism and review, no part of this publication may be reproduced, scanned, or distributed in any form without permission. You are supporting writers and allowing Sunbury Press to continue to publish books for every reader. For information contact Sunbury Press, Inc., Subsidiary Rights Dept., PO Box 548, Boiling Springs, PA 17007 USA or legal@sunburypress.com.

For information about special discounts for bulk purchases, please contact Sunbury Press Orders Dept. at (855) 338-8359 or orders@sunburypress.com.

To request one of our authors for speaking engagements or book signings, please contact Sunbury Press Publicity Dept. at publicity@sunburypress.com.

FIRST SPECKLED EGG PRESS EDITION: June 2025

Interior design by Crystal Devine | Cover and illustrations by Stephanie Miller | Edited by Katie Cressman.

Publisher's Cataloging-in-Publication Data
Names: Garner, Holly, author.
Title: Memory keeper : celebrating and remembering someone we lost and still love / Holly Garner.
Description: First trade paperback edition. | Mechanicsburg, PA : Speckled Egg Press, 2025.
Summary: *Memory Keeper* is a special space just for you, to remember someone you love who is no longer here. You can draw, color, paint, glue, or create new things on the pages . . . whatever feels right for you and your heart. You can also write on the pages in any order you want. This is your space to honor your memories and let your feelings flow freely.
Identifiers: ISBN : 979-8-88819297-9 (paperback).
Subjects: JUVENILE NONFICTION / General | JUVENILE NONFICTION / Activity Books / General | JUVENILE NONFICTION / Activity Books / Coloring.

Designed in the USA
0 1 1 2 3 5 8 13 21 34 55

For the Love of Books!

For Levi,

Someone who will always be remembered for his sense of humor, his smile,
his contagious positive energy, and his love of life.

> Keep memories of your loved one close to your heart
> - one page at a time.

Welcome to your Memory Keeper. This journal is a special space just for you, to remember someone you love. You can draw, color, paint, glue, or create new things on the pages.... Whatever feels right for you and your heart. You can also write on the pages in any order you want. This is your space to honor your memories and let your feelings flow freely.

You may notice that these pages are colorless. The empty space is waiting for you to decorate the pages with your memories. What do you feel as you think about your loved one? Is it a memory that makes you smile or a moment that makes you feel sad? Let your feelings show up in color, in words, or in whatever way helps you express yourself.

And remember, it's okay to feel all sorts of things while you work through your memories. Sadness, anger, happiness, excitement—there are no wrong feelings. What's most important is that you notice them all, because they are part of you, and part of the love you have for the person you've lost.

This journal celebrates

_____

My _____

OUR NICKNAMES FOR EACH OTHER

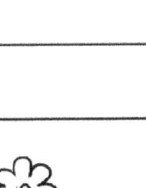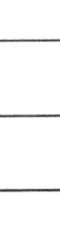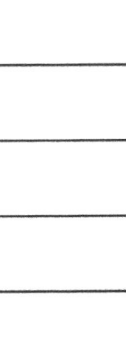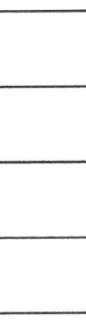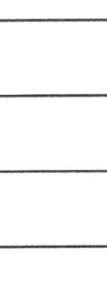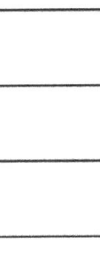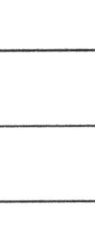

 # Things we both loved

♡ _____

♡ _____

♡ _____

♡ _____

♡ _____

I remember laughing when you...

HAHAHA

Our favorite things to do together...

What I miss most about you...

Here are some things you taught me...

When people ask me about you this is what I tell them...

Words that describe you.....

CREATIVE

Compassionate

Empathetic

Kind

TRUSTWORTHY

Determined

GENEROUS

respectful

Loyal

PATIENT

COURAGEOUS

SMART

Honest

INTEGRITY

As you create your journal, remember that the process of remembering never ends. Through words, colors, and art, you've created a space where your love and emotions for your loved ones can live on. It is important that you continue to take all the time you need and know that the memories you cherish will always have a place in your heart and on these pages.

Remember, this journal is your special space, for you to use however you need. You may choose to share your memory keeper with others who love your loved one like you do or keep it for yourself to treasure. Your love is endless, and this journal will always be a part of that story.

Still battling some big emotions? Consider spending time with our emotion monsters and the Emotion Ensemble series (angry, lonely, frustrated, jealous and sad).

About the Author

Holly Garner has been an educator for over 30 years. Her experience as a teacher, reading specialist, elementary principal, and most importantly, a mom of three boys, helped develop her passion for social emotional learning in schools. Currently, Holly serves as the Director of the Grace B. Luhrs Elementary Lab School and an Associate Professor at Shippensburg University in Pennsylvania. She has written 8 other children's books, including *Letters from Leo*, *More Letters from Leo*, *STUCK*, *Life Lessons From Leo*, and the Emotion Ensemble series.

In her free time, Holly enjoys playing games with her family, playing pickleball, reading on the beach, and planning parties.

About the Illustrator

Stephanie Miller has been an educator for 25 years. Growing up in a creative family inspired her to pursue her passion for painting and drawing. Stephanie is currently a third-grade teacher at Grace B. Luhrs Elementary School in Shippensburg, Pennsylvania.

In her free time, she enjoys visiting her two children, spending time with family, painting, and reading.

Other Books by Holly Garner

The Emotion Ensemble Series

Why is Angry so Angry?
Why is Sad so Sad?
Why is Frustrated so Frustrated?
Why is Jealous so Jealous?
Why is Lonely so Lonely?

STUCK!

Letters from Leo
More Letters from Leo
Life Lessons from Leo

www.ingramcontent.com/pod-product-compliance
Lightning Source LLC
LaVergne TN
LVHW010308070426
835512LV00024B/3482